DO NOT FEAR THE PUPPETEER

A collection of poetry

Paulette Gindi

Published by Poette Publications
ISBN: 9798218254551

Cover design by Liana Moss
Interior layout and design by Paulette Gindi

For questions, requests, or if you feel like sharing your own sacred words of wisdom, feel free to contact the author at the address below:

Poette LLC
P.O. Box 661514
Los Angeles, CA
90066

First Print: September 2023
Printed in the USA

www.thepoette.com

Dedicated to the glorious unknown

"The religion you were born with becomes more important to you as you see the universality of truth."
Ram Dass

se·phi·ra
/səˈfɪrə/
noun
plural noun: **sephiroth**

1. (in cabalism) each of the ten attributes or emanations surrounding the Infinite and by means of which it relates to the finite. They are represented as spheres on the Tree of Life.[1]

---

[1] *Oxford Dictionary*

Author's Note

Growing up in a traditionally Jewish household, I was instilled with the belief that fearing God was one of the ultimate commandments. The teachings of my heritage shaped my understanding of spirituality and guided my path. However, as I embarked on my personal journey, I discovered a burning desire within me to reclaim my power, and to approach Source with more curiosity, rather than fear.

In my quest for meaning, I delved deep into the realms of altered states of consciousness, as well as Jewish mysticism, particularly the Kabbalah. The mystical wisdom of the physical and supernatural realities, as revealed by exploration of consciousness and the Kabbalah, captivated my imagination and filled me with awe. Along this journey, I had the privilege of engaging with scholars, rabbis, shamans, and mystics, learning from their wisdom and experiences. Drawing from these encounters, I have woven my own interpretation of the 10 sephiroth, the mystical spheres that make up the Kabbalistic Tree of Life.

Let me be clear: I do not claim to be an expert in Kabbalah. However, the introduction of the

Zohar (11:2) offers a profound insight that resonates with me:

> "...the moment when a novel interpretation in the Torah is presented by any person, that word ascends and is met before the Holy One. And the Holy One receives this matter and kisses it."[2]

This Kabbalistic verse has become my cosmic permission slip to infuse my poetry with the essence of the Tree of Life. In this poetry collection, I utilize the power of words to traverse the sacred branches, unveiling glimpses of the Divine. Within its pages, you will find the ramblings of the unknown, my explorations of this planet and realms beyond, metaphors of love and grief that transcend earthly boundaries, and rhymes that possess the potential to shift realities.

I have meticulously organized these poetic expressions into the 10 sephiroth, commencing with Keter, the crown, and descending to Malchut, the realm of royalty. Each chapter represents my personal interpretation and

---

[2] *Sefaria.org Community Translation*

intimate relationship with the aspect of the Infinite that it embodies.

Please, pour yourself a cup of cacao, tea, or something else that's warm and nourishing. And as you read, I invite you to explore these realms with an open mind, and even more importantly –an open heart. Breathe it in at your own pace, free your imagination while you paint your own interpretations, and surrender to curiosity.

May these verses awaken within you the same sense of empowerment, healing, and spiritual liberation that I have found. Together, let us cast aside the chains of fear and embrace the puppeteer within ourselves, dancing to the rhythm of our own stories.

With love,
Paulette
Sacred Valley, Peru

"With ten utterances, the world was created."
Pirkei Avot 5:1

And with ten chapters, this book was created.

Keter: Crown
The Great Unknown

Like a majestic crown adorning the head, the first sephira, Keter, radiates with a brilliance that transcends earthly comprehension. This sacred symbol embodies concepts that stretch far beyond the limitations of the human mind. In this chapter, titled *The Great Unknown*, I embark on an exploration of uncharted territories, diving headfirst into the depths of the enigmatic and the ineffable. Through poetic prose, I invite you to join me on a journey of discovery, where the familiar gives way to the extraordinary and the boundaries of perception expand. Together, let us unravel the mysteries that lie within the realm of the crown.

"We came from a dark abyss, we end in a dark abyss, and we call the luminous interval life."
Nikos Kazantzakis

AH

reincarnated onto this sphere
and controlled by a Puppeteer
some people call
Jah, Krishna, Allah, Pachamama

maybe these names for our maker are hinting at
us to scream

AH

maybe the only law
enforced upon us is to sing
instead of obsessively worshiping
the One who pulls the strings

a remake of plato's allegory of the cave

what's the source of consciousness?

i find myself seeking an answer amongst the
bottomless
ocean
sinking into the currents,
resisting the motions

i attempt to swim to shore,
to steady ground
but am swept away and am drowned

i reincarnate into a simple fish
and ask myself,
"i wonder if there's more than this sea abyss?"

my fish friends call me crazy,
saying water is all there is –
that the purpose of life is to flourish

right then and there,
a seagull catches me from the sea and brings me
up in the air
i see the grand water and the sand
all my fish life i knew there was such thing as land

before i can savor it,
i am dropped back into the water
now a bit more mentally stronger

i tell my friends – there's such thing as land!
but they don't understand

they say i'm delusional
but i continue on and share how beautiful
the sun hits the sea
and how there is such a thing as palm trees!

they laugh and say i'm insane
that underwater is the only terrain

so i begin to question
that glimpse of the other side
and start to think
that perhaps my eyes had just lied

that deep in the sea is all there is
and to swim and to flourish is why i exist

the choice of living

my near death experience
made me quite delirious

left this world for what seemed like

                                    infinity

experienced what it means
to be free from misery

returned to this body
my reason for being here a little bit foggy

felt like i didn't belong
as if everything i once believed in
had been wrong

started to believe
that i am nothing but a puppet
and there was no life goal
to summit

this entire reality become nothing but a game
played by something,
some people call
"The Name"

i wanted to break free from its control
so i started to go down alice's rabbit hole

believing that i am nothing but a lie
wanting nothing more but to die

~

i then remembered
poetry
the beauty of a redwood tree
the taste of aged sticky rice tea
the saltiness of the mediterranean sea
reminisced about the coral reefs i have yet to see

so i figured,
i may not actually be free
but this simulation can be quite pretty

so i chose to let myself be

arrive to be alive

visitors to this earth
transported here through the canal of birth

don't remember what came before reality
how we all came to be creatures of vitality

i do believe
we've agreed to participate in this dimension
even though we don't have the comprehension

                and i must admit
                some days i want to quit

and return to that cosmic place
where i feel embraced

but i trust that i will return back when i am called

until then

                i live a life enthralled

ode to the toad

oh dear sonoran desert toad
you make my heart explode
into infinite fractals of universal cosmic dust
you are the one i trust
whispering secrets that go beyond this realm's
wallpaper
so i may connect to my maker
and realize it's been me all along
showing me that i belong
on this sphere
that i am both puppet and puppeteer
oh dear sonoran desert toad
thank you for the wisdom you have bestowed

do not fear the Puppeteer

hanging on
      by the threads of the Puppeteer's strings

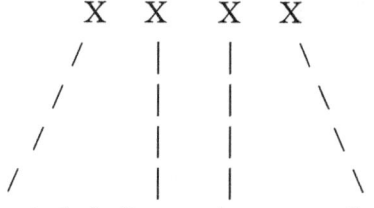

       naively believing that we are free

          and have

             >wings<

thinking that we possess free will
that we have a mission to fulfill

but perhaps this play we participate in
is just a script
and that our Director has us   w h i p p e d
to act as It pleases –
that we are just pieces
of the Writers's imagination

      She created earth
      and titled it 'creation'

we are blind to see
that we are nothing but actors
in a thriller film
with too many chapters

deep down we know the ending
but for some reason
we cannot remember

stuck in a character,
experiencing an adventure
waiting for the Divine to shout

"CUT!"

Chochma: Wisdom
Beginning In Time

Within the realms of Chochma, the second sephira, wisdom emerges like a primordial force, igniting the fires of creation. In this chapter, titled *Beginning In Time*, I delve into the essence of wisdom and its role in shaping our relationship to time. Through poetic expressions, I explore the timeless insights that bridge the gap between the infinite and the finite. Time has become a poetic muse that inspires me to tap into the wellspring of wisdom and delve into the depths of the temporary.

"Teach us to number our days,
so that we may gain a heart of wisdom."
Psalms 90:12

trust the dust

don't underestimate
the power of falling apart

the universe had to explode
into infinite particles
just for us to experience
this exact moment in time

once upon a now

this moment was
once
a prayer
and this moment shall become a
once
upon a time

the afterlife of every moment

you and i
both know
the old doesn't die

people, places, memories, lessons
don't just disappear with time
they transition and reach ascension
some – reincarnation
and others transition from
longing into rhyme

shifts between breaths

and it's like everything is
changing in numbers

the date on the calendar
the temperature of the air
the ocean level
the prices of the market
the amount of lines on my forehead
the distance between me and home

and it's like everything is
changing in numbers

yet everything is
the same kind of *numb*

houdini

moments will do
what moments
do best –
disappear.

another second wiser

i write these lines on this sheet
and in return
am given another line on my cheek

a g i n g

i am aging

breath by breath
inches me closer to
death

be here now

time
doesn't stand still
but
stillness
stands in time

crypto crash and every other kind of crash

no matter how hard you try
a picked flower will always die
because this too shall pass
the beauty and the ugly
all the pain as well as what feels lovely
will wilt away in just a flash
so will this crash

medicine of reminisce

i don't need to remember to write
i write to remember –
to surrender
to the memory.

    the pain of yesterday
     only has one remedy:

          to remember

            then let go

6 steps to realize that all is temporary

1. write poetry to realize magical things take time
2. visit mauna kea to realize it is safe to sit in stillness for millennia
3. drink an entire mug of cacao to realize beautiful vessels can be empty too
4. create art past sunset to realize colors exist in the darkness
5. watch sea turtles to realize it is okay to get lost in the currents
6. read this chapter again to realize everything has an ending

Binah: Understanding
I Am

Binah, the third sephira, beckons us to delve into the realm of understanding, where the enigmatic becomes clear. In this chapter, *I Am*, I explore the intricacies of self-awareness and the power of deep understanding of ego. Through poetic musings, I unravel the mysteries that lie within our own being, peeling back the layers to reveal the essence of who we truly are. *I Am* navigates the labyrinth of introspection and identity.

"I am not what happened to me,
I am what I choose to become."
Carl Jung

pereskia

blossoming into a flower
reclaiming my power

don't come close
for i am not a rose

don't come near
for i am no shakespeare

i am blossoming into a flower
but i am not to be appreciated by a coward

for i am sitting on top of a cactus

seeker

i am a seeker
and every person i meet is my teacher
shining a light on the spaces
that need my attention
so i may rise above and reach my ascension

i am a seeker
and sometimes i question
how i became this wild creature
did my essence agree
to participate in this simulation?
or is the idea of even having an "essence"
just part of the collective imagination?

i am a seeker
and i want to go within
a bit deeper
to understand the make up
of this body's existence
so i may tell my suffering
good riddance

i am a seeker
and to be honest,
i don't even know what i'm looking for
i am just so used to waging war

unable to accept the status quo
always seeking
to escape the sensation of slow

i am a seeker
and everyday
this body becomes a little bit weaker
losing sight
of my intentions of being in this dimension
awaiting for my soul's exodus' redemption

i am a seeker
i am also a dreamer
and a believer
that there's a purpose that expands
beyond these eyes
and i may not see it now,
but i will understand
when this body dies.

reincarnation

these jungle bites leave me swollen
i laugh at the thought of these flying critters
roaming into the wilderness filled with me
is this what it means to be reincarnated as a forest
fairy?
perhaps so

oh, how i've taken crazy for granted

i miss standing at the
                          edge
                              of insanity

because there i had the view
of the most profound poetry

i am now on safe ground
trying to get lost
because
fuck being found.

i am sea

sometimes i am stuck in the inbetween
sometimes i am freer than my own imagination
sometimes i feel like a queen
sometimes i feel like a puppet in a simulation
sometimes i feel small and fragile
sometimes i feel like a warrior
sometimes i love to travel
sometimes i cling on to the same door
sometimes i am swimming with the motions
sometimes i am drowning in the currents
all the time, i am the entire ocean.

note to self when i feel like i am not enough

1. no need to buy stuff
2. be gentle, not rough
3. let go of the image of tough
4. you are the locksmith to that handcuff

Chesed: Love
In Through The Heart

Traditionally translated to "kindness" or "loving-kindness", at its core, the fourth sephira, Chesed, emanates love. *In Through The Heart* is a journey of exploring the entire spectrum of love – from grief to ecstasy.

"The whole universe is through and through the playing of love in every shade of the word's use, from animal lust to divine charity."
Alan Watts

the answer

is always love.

love thy earth

let's bring the system down to its knees
give some loving to the soil and the trees
rid the plastic from our sacred seas
respect the bees
our earth cannot afford anymore degrees
it's about time we help antarctica refreeze
let's stop funding war,
and start educating on peace

it is now or never
let's plant the seeds.

hand wash only

i told him hand wash only
that i am a vibrant, delicate fabric
that needs gentle care
that i need to be washed with pure castile soap
under lukewarm water
and hung on a wooden hanger in the front yard

but instead

he threw me in the washing machine
on high and hot
my colors fading
my textures tainting
he didn't care at all
he never planned on wearing me again anyways

embrace me, do not change me

they say i am the author of my life
and i can't help but to question:
why do i look for romance
like i'm hiring an editor?
when lovers are just readers

,

i was hoping you'd become my ending
that we'd walk into the jungle sunset
hand in hand
sweat in sweat
flying off into the distance
like hungry mosquitos
feeding off one another for eternity to come

but you are not my ending
not even a chapter
our connection was as brief as a comma between
two words in a simple sentence
fleeting, but necessary.

the final union

i want to rise from a dream
only to be living a fairytale
in the arms of a beloved
drinking cacao
overlooking a panorama i have yet to witness
we'd laugh about the almost forevers
and be grateful for the unpaved roads
that led to our union

me first

i loved you
so i held onto you

i love myself
so i let you go

f a s t

not sure what runs the fastest:
my mind,
your feet,
time.

slow

not sure what moves the slowest:
my healing,
your hands,
time.

you won't see this

i will make you into poetry you will never read
dress you up in gentle rhymes
and ink that bleeds
put you in a random chapter of some collection
make you look like perfection
i'll publish you for the entire world to see
how beautiful you are
when you become poetry

all the love in the world

you don't need
to compete
for their love
because
all the love
that you seek
is already at your feet
reminding you
that you are always complete

virginia tobacco stuffed corn cob pipe

you say smoking
is the closest our lips will ever get to fire
but the goodbye
that drips off your tongue
begs to differ

body language

touch
isn't my
love language
it is my
native tongue

an unopened love letter

i broke myself free from their box
only to neatly fold myself up
to fit in an envelope
hoping
it would end up in his mailbox

again and again

walking this earth is intense
because i have no defense
i put my heart on the table from the start
the moment i meet you, i turn you into art
it is both a blessing and a curse
that i am obsessed
with putting love into a verse

addicted to the painkiller

i try to numb my loneliness with your touch

i know it isn't honest
but i just need to feel the rush

when you leave in the morning
i feel the wound burning

aching from the heart in so much pain
i then remember
sex and bandaids aren't the same

one poem closer to letting go

while you drink to forget
i write to remember

you go off and drown your pain
inside a glass of whiskey
while i wipe my tears
with this sheet of poetry

glass after glass
numbing

word after word
healing

inhale that real shit

you deserve love that gives you breath,
not love that takes your breath away.

full of hope and you

i am filled with hope
as the ocean is filled with raindrops
as earth is filled with soil
as music is filled with melody
as pleasure is filled with pain
as i am filled with you

nona

had i known that would be the last time

i would have accepted
another bite of your cooking
would have glanced
into your hazel eyes a breath longer
would have taken
my sweet time
walking towards
and out
of your front door

stop waiting to love yourself

for so long i was slowly drowning
as my heart was frantically pounding

being suffocated by this massive cold wave
shouting out for love to come and save

and amidst the waiting
and the unpredictable ocean
i realized that my fins may be small,
but they are not broken

and all that i need
has been at my fingertips all along
i just needed to make them a little bit more
strong

i started off slow,
and immediately started to grow
i learned how to swim
and immersed myself
in the love that is eternally within

Gevurah: Power
Rise

Gevurah, the fifth sephira, unleashes the mighty power within us, inviting us to rise above limitations and embrace our inner strength. *Rise* explores my fierce determination to create my own story, rise above religious and societal conditionings, and take my power back.

"Let me fall if I must fall.
The one I will become will catch me."
Baal Shem Tov

to rise in joy

she began to
dance
instead of
running

stopped trying to
survive
and began
living

beyond any shape

i sometimes miss the box that i've outgrown
because at least then,
i felt like i had a home

i built myself a castle
only to realize
i am no damsel

i want to be free from all structures
i want to embrace
the wildness of my divinely creature

no more confining
only aligning
to the highest of highs

i am here to rise
out off every shape
i've put myself into

dear mom

do not tame me
or i will break free
i will become a stormy sea
loading my reckless waves with poetry

do not put me in a box
i was not born to live a life that is orthodox
i was put here to be wild
playful and careless as a child

do not tell me how to love
or who to love
or who to worship
i no longer follow your script

heaven is here

my freedom
was realized
when i began
to live
for the moment
rather than
the afterlife

cannibalism vs capitalism

in a war with one another through capitalism
ravaging our brothers and sisters like it's
cannibalism
all for another digit
forgetting that we are here just to visit
and that when we return
our last concern
will be a number on a screen
but rather how much love we've held in our
being

flee to be free

"it is time to wed"
they said

so instead
i fled

jeru-salam

salam shalom
two nations
one home

        iron
        dome
        of the rock

if only it were as simple as this poem

illusions of capitalist institutions

when it's all been said and done
and you return to One
you will see what it's all been worth

understanding the reason of your birth
so don't keep your treasures here on earth

when you return to One
after you've had your fun
you won't be able to take the keys to your
treasure chest
you'll be left with nothing but rest

shedding skin

ready to release
all that is holding me back
from peace

(ie. the need to please,
chasing the treasure chest's keys,
unrequited love to seize, ect...)

shatra شاطرة

living inside gloom
my mother swears the solution is to find a groom
so i can take a broom
and sweep every room
of the house
and be the perfect spouse

breaking tradition

my ancestors
didn't survive
exile after exile
just
for me
to live a life
that is anything
less than
worthwhile

a non-conforming haiku

it is what it is
no need to be like the rest
melting expectations

27

you are my muse
and i haven't even met you
in the carnation realm

you've gifted me your name
and i've gifted you the freedom it never had

at 27, you were a mother to four,
plus one who slipped away too soon
at 27, i am a mother to words
in a language you wouldn't have understood

at 27, your torso was marked with motherhood
at 27, my torso is marked with ink

at 27, you have never stepped foot
outside of your village
at 27, i am roaming
uncharted territory

i've never met you in this carnation realm
but i know you're proud of me

hasta la vista l.a.

plastic pleasures
chasing treasures
everyone's strangers
city of angels

from synagogues to meditation halls

"my way or the highway"
mom would say

so i ran away
and chose the high way

leviticus 19:28

i ink this skin
they say it is a sin
as if it is a reflection
of the purity of the soul within

they say it is permanent
but what is permanence
other than a brief moment?

all of my conditionings and fears
spiral out of control
trying to remember that i am not a body –
i am soul

this form is nothing but a vessel
that aids my essense to ascend to a higher level

all of this is temporary,
this inked body and the memories i carry
will be laid with me in a cemetery

so do not say it is a sin
that i cherish and embellish this skin.

hustle culture

move like you are moving through
honey

oh dear,

you are worth more than any amount of
money

giving it my all

i am so done with playing small
it is time for me to rise and stand tall
knock down the wall
follow my inner call

and trust that i will be caught
if i fall

Tiferet: Beauty
Embrace the Face of Light

Tiferet, the sixth sephira, radiates with the divine beauty that permeates all aspects of existence. *Embrace the Face of Light* is a poetic exploration of the profound beauty that is around and within. Through lyrical verses, I celebrate the harmonious interplay of discovering my beauty, cultivating balance, compassion, and aesthetic splendor. *Embrace the Face of Light* immerses ourselves in the breathtaking tapestry of life, discovering the inherent light that resides within ourselves and the world.

"A little bit of light dispels a lot of darkness. "
Rabbi Schneur Zalman

same juice, different vessel

want you to see beyond
this face
this body
this hair
no need to compare
your light to mine
we are each a manifestation of divine
regardless of color or texture
when we take off this human costume
we are all the same creature
created from the same well
placed on the same spell
that has kept us blind to see
that what's inside of you
is what's inside of me.

we are what we seek

i've been chasing god
like a puppy chasing its tail

running away
to sacred ruins
without digging up the soil
behind my own house

i've been reading scriptures
in an unfamiliar alphabet
without reading the lines
on my palm

been drinking plants
revered by others
without tasting
the holy juices secreted by my eyes

been chanting choruses
of indigenous tribes
without singing
my own story

so i asked my heart,
how do i embrace
my own heritage,

my own song,
my own medicine?

and heart told me,
through not fearing the puppeteer,
and sharing these pages
for all to see.

life-bound friend

looking at my reflection
for so long, all i saw back was imperfection

               mistakes
               shattered dreams
               unworthiness

i filled the woman looking back with kindness

               fed her affirmation
               validation
               motivation

and watched her
        transformation
from imperfect to perfect

she now carries so much respect
for her life-bound friend named body

kinhin

walk as if your feet are kissing the earth
walk as if you know your soul's worth
walk as if this life is your only birth

more than skin

afraid to show this skin
sometimes i prefer you just love me for the within
rather than the mask i was given at birth

i wish that the first
thing you see is my divine flame
rather than a face to a name

manifestation of the divine

looking at my reflection in the mirror,
all of my flaws becoming a blur
seeing divine's beauty in human form
no need to perform

tzununa during feria

i don't want to be like fireworks
synthetically lighting up the sky
just for entertainment –

i want to be like lightning

lighting up the sky
unexpectedly,
startling,
knocking down anything that gets in my way.

Netzach: Victory
Surrender to the Shadow

Netzach, the seventh sephira, pulsates with the energy of victory, inviting us to confront our shadows and emerge triumphant. *Surrender to the Shadow* explores the depths of the human experience, exploring the transformative power of shadow work. Through poetic musings, I celebrate the triumphs that arise from the darkest corners of life, while leading my own way towards self-growth. Join me as we navigate the intricate dance between light and shadow, embracing the victories that await us on the other side.

"One does not become enlightened by imagining figures of light, but by making the darkness conscious."
Carl Jung

keep going

do not run
from this new chapter that has begun
the beginning may seem scary
it may not always feel merry
but the universe has guided you here for
a reason
so fight that demon
that whispers in your ear
to turn back around
stand your ground
you've got this

transformation

sit with your ugly
until it turns lovely

dear wanderer

your feet
graze
the external
in hopes of
discovering
the internal

have you been counting
the sunrises?
or are you
too busy
counting the sunsets,
collecting goodbyes
waiting for the right amount
until you embark to
a new destination?

cosmic bypassing

you can run as far as your tired feet will allow
but wherever you go,
there will be your shadow
and if you want to free yourself
from this vicious cycle
you need to let go of the denial
and to acknowledge these patterns
and stop blaming them on the
astrological positioning of saturn

nomadic commandment: thou shall be the puppeteer

when i was a child
i was taught that
the holiest thing one can do
is fear
the one who puppeteers

and like a child,
when fear
is here,
natural impulse is to run

and now like a child
i am running from place to place
unable to settle down
because i fear
the one i meet
again and again

water me

tenderness
should not be mistaken for weakness
gentle petals
with a thorny stem
through the blood and the admiration
she continues to grow
and thanks the ~~rain~~ pain
for giving her stronger roots

imposter fyndrome

i left my fishbowl for the ocean
and now i'm living in constant motion
wave after wave
unsure if i can be so brave
swimming amongst the sharks and whales
feeling self-conscious about my scales
missing my fishbowl
the zone where i felt so whole
now i dabble in constant doubt
desire to jump out
struggling to trust that i will grow
afraid to swim slow
the most i can do is polish my own scales
instead of focusing on everyone else's strong tails
letting go of my attachment to dry ground
and trusting that i will not drown

virtual galaxy

embracing diversions, my favored stance,
an excuse for inaction, a tempting dance.
within this virtual galaxy, i find solace,
obscuring truths, reality's face.
anything to evade my inner strife,
avoiding healing, evading life.
reasons i concoct, a multitude untold,
ignoring my soul's whispers, growing bold.
deeper i sink, in existential abyss,
distractions embraced, a temporary bliss.
for in these fleeting moments, dissatisfaction
fades,
yet, my soul's longing remains unswayed.

shadow dance

you can tiptoe around the broken

      g   s
          l a   s

but what's the point if you can't dance?

a new journey

i've been running away from the dark
ever since i could walk
unable to surrender to the discomfort
which in my terms,
is anything under triumphant
the moment shadow creeps in
is when i begin
to pack my bags
and without any solid plans
i get up,
move along
and journey somewhere new,
hoping i will belong.

spiritual bypassing

if you're so obsessed with the idea of becoming "one"
then become one with your discomfort

merge into the dark unknown
until it starts to feel like home

fuck shadow work

every flower needs
both the sun and the rain to grow
but i am a cactus
desire for nothing but sunshine

the wildness of earth and me

into the wilderness i go
attempting to escape the boring
forever on a mission of exploring
everything and anything that is outside of me
because i feel like i don't have the courage to see
the depths of my own internal sea

no mud, no lotus

thud thud
heart beats in the mud

discomfort deep down
yet she never frowns

she trusts the process
as she enters metamorphosis

hocus pocus
she transforms into a blue lotus

dance / listen

sometimes life is about
being able to dance with
the music
the screams
the silence

and

sometimes life is about
taking a seat in the corner
and without judgment,
listen to
the music
the screams
the silence

no shortcuts

there are no shortcuts here
it's not like you get to skip over fear

you can't bypass
the displeasure
and expect for the detour to
lead you to treasure

you need to go through every winding road
to get to the place that is your gold

Hod: Awe
Wonderful Mystery

Hod, the eighth sephira, reveals the awe-inspiring mysteries that lie at the heart of existence. *Wonderful Mystery* is an ode to the beautiful unknown of life and Earth. During my travels, I have had poetic reflections that have inspired me to celebrate the intricate interplay of knowledge and humility, unraveling the secrets that awaken a sense of wonder within me. Hod is a reminder that our senses are just a fraction of what exists. May the wonders of the Universe continue to inspire art and curiosity.

"The most beautiful thing we can experience is the mysterious. It is the source of all true art and science."
Albert Einstein

ocean

all rivers lead to you
even the ones i've basked in
far away from you
against you
opposite of you
in the depths of valleys
and at altitudes of 11,000 feet above you

every single one i've met
is just a limb of you
in disguise

is that how god works too?

ground down or keep flying?

"what bird would you be?" he asks
and i can't make up my mind

to be a hummingbird
flying low
saturated by the juicy flowers
and humans
who choose to live in harmony with me

or

to be a vulture
flying high
and experiencing the gift of distance
witnessing the diversity of humans
that vary from village to village

/oh mauna loa\

v
o l
cano\
oozing
fertile soil
for mana to
grow / teach me
to go s l o w \
living for n o w \ no
promises of tomorrow \ you
leave me speechless, nothing but
w o w \ remind me all that i already
know / that all this earth is just for us to
borrow / no fire to force, just immerge in
flow / oh sweet vessel of flames, there's liquid
earth below / and above a   r a i n bow

tasty mystery

i delight in the enigma, akin to the act
of partaking in a luscious pomegranate's essence.

unfolding its succulent nature, i indulge,
bewitched by the myriad of 613 seed-born
prospects.

with reverence, i savor each exquisite finger,
caressing them with my tongue,
imbibing the nectar's saccharine allure,
conveyed upon my lips with utmost reverence.

no seed shall be unveiled in vain,
for i relish this riddle, resplendent in its majesty.

california // these are a few of my favorite things

pine resin
authentic expression
linen paper
the smell of amber
beeswax candles
open toe sandals
peppermint tea
poetry
tulsi beads
redwood trees
big sur
myrrh
embodied movement
living in the present

storm

how do i be as loud as thunder?
how do i light up the darkness like lightning?
how do i be loved like rain during a drought?

the tallest mountain on earth

mother nature
is our greatest teacher

look at the rain
showing us that it's okay to release pain

look at winter
gently whispering
to slow down,
rest,
and tend to the inner

look at earthquakes
taking its time

      one
      after
      another

         s l o w l y

            forming
               mauna kea

grand canyon

i am not a temple
nor a church
not a lily
nor a rose
not mt everest
nor the dead sea

i am the grand canyon
deep, mysterious, and very open.

mama

i remember getting lost
in grocery stores as a child
i had fear of never seeing mom again

i'd look down every aisle
until i saw her big blonde hair
and i'd sigh in relief
and wrap my arms around her,
promising myself to never get lost again.

and now, i am still a child
getting lost around the globe

looking down every
river stream and volcano opening

until i see her rocks, dirt, and leaves,
and i'd sigh in relief
and wrap my arms around her
thanking her for the birth of all of existence.

2023 syrian earthquake

aleha hashalom
may peace be upon you

within your bones
and upon the land in which you lay

your ribcage, which once held your heart
fractured by humanity above

your vertebrae vibrating by the ripples of earth
in which we all came from

your pelvis, once a home for eight bodies
is now giving birth to its ninth named hope

aleha hashalom
may you rest within peace

even when your bones quake
from both war and mother nature

18 names of goddess

shape shifter
ocean gifter
breath mover
body groover
tongue twister
unknown sister
ground shaker
love maker
silent rhythm
internal vision
melody tuner
nighttime lunar
humming sensation
deep meditation
glowing radiance
infinite abundance
magical witchery
wonderful mystery

Yesod: Foundation
State to Create

Yesod, the ninth sephira, serves as the foundation upon which our dreams take shape and manifest into reality. In this chapter titled *State to Create*, I explore the power of imagination, dreaming, womanhood, and the creative forces that shape our lives. Through poetic expressions, I celebrate the transformative potential that lies within us, inviting us to tap into the wellspring of the collective creative energy.

"You can't use up creativity.
The more you use, the more you have."
Maya Angelou

creativity

you are divinity
cosmic creativity
that is beyond productivity
so reach for infinity
all that you desire is of possibility
if you can dream it, it is in proximity.

the journey of creating poetry

these stanzas have been written
by a wide-eyed wanderer
who searched across oceans
to find the right arrangement of the alphabet

father's father

i remember you
like
i remember
my dreams

a forgotten memory
that i know was mesmerizing

creator, you are

your life is yours to create

will you fill it up with love
or with hate?
will you say it's all coincidence
or will you say it's fate?
will you go after your dreams
or sit around and wait?
take the path of curves
or the one that is straight?

your life is yours to create
not yours to waste

beyond the pill

i have a desire to connect to my sacral center
that sacred space where a new soul can enter

within her vastness comes creation
of ideas, love-making and baby manifestation

she feels neglected of her divine power
thirsty for self to water her flower

to pray and to heal the accumulated wounds
and to finally align her
to the rhythm of the moon

these words fertilize her soil so she may shine
and return to her natural state, which is sublime.

freedom to create

butterfly in a beehive
trying to survive
the stings
that are weighing down my w
                              i
                              n
                              g
                              s

unsure how i made my way in here
the journey seems so unclear

i want to set myself free
before dying drenched in h
                              o
                              n
                              e
                              y

i want to set myself free
because there is still some poetry
i have yet to offer your eyes to see

puna summer 2022

they call this paradise ~
lava cliffs overlooking the pacific
bushes offering lilikoi
rainbow piercing clouds
and an abundance of moisturizer gifted by
goddess humidity

but when i think of paradise ~
i think of lava flowing from you into me
my bush offering you a different kind of
sweetness
rainbows reflected from your eyes into mine
and an abundance of moisturizer gifted by love

cosmic sculpture

fuck being your masterpiece
i just want to be a master of peace

i am no longer trying
to fit on a canvas
no longer minimizing
my complexities for you to understand

i am a work of art that
exceeds the sheet and the canvas
i am a work of art that
is beyond shapes and colors

if you can't carry me home,
then too bad
i don't belong on your bedroom wall anyways

preservation

i write poetry
to keep the temporary
places, experiences, and people
alive a bit longer
past
their expiration date

the intersection of connection

there is no separation
between the
last page and this one
love and pain
poet and reader
puppet and puppeteer

all is connected
by the invisible threads of existence

nueva

what is new to me
is an opportunity
for me to plant some seeds
and manifest my wildest of dreams

sameness

i write poetry
to heal
i write poetry
because for so long i was afraid to feel
i write poetry
to reveal
my scars
and to wear them with pride
i write poetry
so you can see my inside
and realize it looks the same as yours
so you may see that we share the same sores

all ways within

"wow, i didn't know i had that in me"
i think as
i dance
i cry
i laugh
i give away love
i write poetry

Malchut: Royalty
Welcome to the Queendom

In the realm of Malchut, the tenth sephira, we embark on a poetic exploration of femininity, royalty, and being alive. *Welcome to the Queendom* integrates the first nine spheres of the Tree of Life and grounds it down into this three-dimensional world. Within these verses, we celebrate the majestic qualities that grace the feminine spirit, illuminating the world with its radiance. We delve into a regality that transcends mere crowns and castles, embracing the unique power and beauty inherent in every individual, reminding us of our divine lineage. Let these words inspire you to embrace your own royal nature, recognizing the splendor of the tapestry we weave as humans.

"Freeing yourself was one thing,
claiming ownership
of that freed self was another."
Toni Morrison

welcome to the queendom

take your shoes off before you enter
move slowly, for she is tender
oh my, what a splendor
once you meet her,
you won't have a choice but to surrender

a wordless form of poetry
sweeter than the juiciest cherry
multi-limbed sanctuary
her body

her touch feels like home
she is confident beyond her throne
unafraid for her wounds to be shown
everywhere her feet walk is her queendom

you are queen

stop waiting for permission
this life is your decision
go on and live your mission
tap into your inherent wisdom
and create your own queendom

royal manifestations

like a waterfall
she is not here to water you

she may be beautiful
but if you disrespect her, she may drown you

like a warrior
she dances with a sword in her hand

keeps warm with her own fur
protects her sacred land

like a queen
she listens and she nurtures
does not need to be seen

for all she desires, becomes hers

blessed

she continues to keep her heart open
but don't be fooled,
for she won't settle for almost chosen

wears her heart on her sleeve
but she doesn't need to please

she walks this earth
as if her feet are made of glass

she takes it slowly,
doesn't understand the purpose of fast

step   by   step

                              breath by   breath

she moves with intention
as if she is constantly experiencing
divine intervention

she has the strength to carry
all of the love in just one hand
not afraid for her mind to expand

she doesn't hold on to yesterday

she continues on the path
her own way

she is fearless
unafraid to express
no one to impress

she is blessed.

About the Author

Paulette Gindi is a writer, artist, and seeker, scouring every corner of her mind, heart, and this planet in search of her next poetic muse. She has devoted many years to cultivating creative liberation for people from all walks of life. She calls Earth her home, but her P.O. Box happens to be in Los Angeles, California.